To Jessica,

Thankyou for
Survey- enjoy this read e learning

Lindsay Taylor

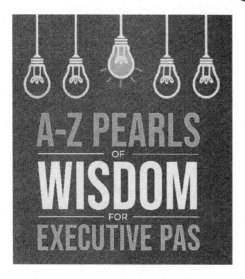

A – Z Pearls of Wisdom for Executive PAs: second edition

First published by Your Excellency Limited, The Lodge, Bath Place,
Clifton, Bedfordshire SG17 5HE, UK. www.yourexcellency.co.uk.

Photographs © Nick Fewings 2015

Edited by Angela Garry (angelagarry@picaaurum.com)

First published 2015. Second edition: 2022.

ISBN: 9798848848373

Printed and bound by www.kdp.amazon.com

Table of Contents

Introduction and message from the author

Hello! I'm Lindsay Taylor, Co-Founder and Director of Your Excellency Limited. We specialise in learning and development for the EA, PA and Administrative Professional. We pride ourselves on providing down-to-earth, fun and beneficial learning, helping you to be *truly exceptional*.

I've collated a wealth of input from professionals across the world in response to my questions "What is an Executive PA?" and "What skills and attributes are needed to be an effective and efficient Executive PA?".

I understand the diversity of the PA role – how it can differ from organisation to organisation, from sector to sector, from team to team. That's what makes the role so exciting. It's also what makes the role so challenging. More and more organisations are realising the worth of their EAs and PAs. You are being welcomed as a valued member of the management team – with this status comes the need for specific skills and attributes, specific Pearls of Wisdom – that are crucial for your overall success.

I've pulled together these Pearls of Wisdom in a useful A-Z format which I know Executive PAs and Administrative Professionals across the world will find not only useful and beneficial, but essential in today's demanding business environment.

You can find out more about our learning and development opportunities on our website at www.yourexcellency.co.uk.

I'd like to say a huge "THANK YOU" to the following:

- My husband, son and daughter for their support and feedback.
- Angela Garry of Pica Aurum for invaluable self-publishing knowledge and pulling this book into the amazing format you see now.
- DeskDemon.com for featuring the original Pearls of Wisdom on their website and for providing a fantastic resource for PAs.
- Nick Fewings who provides the images to complement each Pearl of Wisdom (more of Nick's images can be viewed on his Flickr work-stream www.flickr.com/photos/jannerboy62).
- My friends and clients across the world who have provided testimonials to endorse this book,

And, of course,

- A heartfelt thanks to YOU – the dedicated EAs, PAs and Administrative Professionals who I have the absolute pleasure to work with.

Thank you all.

Lindsay Taylor x

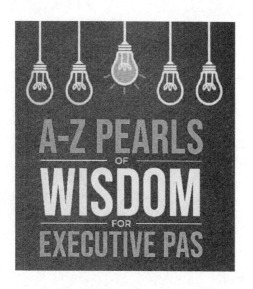

"I will blink before you do"   Few Peeps©

A is for Assertiveness

A is for...Assertiveness

A top ask and want of EAs and PAs, consider Assertiveness to be as simple as ABC, per the Model below.

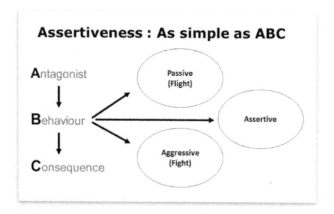

In challenging situations where you are (A) Antagonised by an (A) Antagonist, you are likely to (B) Behave in one of two ways, either Aggressively or Passively.

This is the fight (Aggressive) or flight (Passive) response when we feel threatened. Neither an Aggressive or Passive Behaviour has positive (C) Consequences and it is likely to lose you the respect of your team members and impact your credibility.

Recognise that *you always have a choice of behaviour...* and the very best (B) Behaviour with more positive (C) Consequences is Assertiveness.

What is "assertiveness"?

For me, it's about standing up for what you think and what you believe in, at the same time respecting the fact that not everyone will think the same as you do.

People have different perspectives – everyone "ticks" differently. We are all unique in the way we are made-up.

This is what makes the world such an exciting place to be. This is what makes the world such a challenging place to be.

How do we respond and communicate assertively?

Based on the research of former Harvard Professor Albert Mehrabian, when sharing our thought, feelings and attitudes face to face, we can break down communication into three elements (the 3Vs), namely:

1) Verbal – the words that we speak
2) Vocal – the tone that we use and
3) Visual – the body language that we display.

Mehrabian skewed the Verbal versus non-Verbal elements of communication in his research and attributed percentages to the elements in terms of the importance of communication:

> Verbal accounts for 7% importance,
>
> Vocal 38% importance, and
>
> Visual 55%.

If we use Mehrabian's research in terms of responding assertively then it is clear that we need to pay attention to *how* we deliver our assertive message as well as considering the actual words and Verbal element.

I am an advocate of the saying "failing to plan is planning to fail" – so where possible take time to plan your assertive response.

You can think about your response in terms of The 3Vs with the following "checklists":

Assertive Verbal:

*   Be open, honest and to the point.
*   Use "I" statements – this is about your view.
*   Share your feelings – take ownership of the fact that we are emotional beings.
    Say "I feel...." and claim the emotion you are feeling.
*   Acknowledge your own rights, wants and needs.
*   Ask questions of others to find out their wants and needs.
*   Empathise with the other person's views and respect the fact that people are different and have different views.
*   Focus on problem solving, moving forward and thinking about the future.
    The ideal outcome for any assertive response is for a win-win situation.
    Propose a way forward and then "bounce" this back to your recipient asking them what they think.

Assertive Vocal

- Think about *how* you say the words.
- Speak the meaning, not just the words.
- Think about the timing of your response – put your own view forward and allow others to have their say.
- Ensure your breathing is relaxed and steady.
- Use evenly spaced words.
- Speak at an even pace.
- Use your tone to emphasise key words.

Assertive Visual

- Ensure your eye contact is direct, relaxed and gentle.
- Deliver your message at the same eye level to your recipient(s).
- Keep your posture upright and balanced ("plant" your feet firmly on the ground – so you feel truly "grounded").
- Ensure you face the other person and at the same time respect their personal space.
- Ensure your gestures are balanced and open.
- Ensure your facial expression is open and pleasant.

Assertiveness Aura

In addition I believe assertiveness is at its most powerful when you achieve an Assertiveness Aura – a state of being, a presence, an aura that comes from your belief in yourself – the belief that you are entitled to be assertive, that your opinion is valued and deserves the respect of others.

The 'A' Pearl:

> *"Say what you mean and
> mean what you say."*
> *Lindsay Taylor*

"Framing the Day Ahead"   Few Peeps©

B is for Beliefs

B is for... Beliefs (Your Mind is Your Kingdom)

16th Century English Poet Francis Quarles famously stated *"my mind is my kingdom"*.

If we take time to think about Quarles' meaning, in essence we are creating a rich kingdom in our own minds and ironically substantiating his claim and statement.

Interpreting Quarles' quote further, if we consider our mind to be our own kingdom we are ultimately the "King" or "Queen" of our domain. We have complete control and authority of it — we can rule our kingdom as we see fit — but do we?

Understanding the power of our own thinking and "tapping" into our mind can be highly beneficial, indeed a necessity, in being successful in our everyday lives and achieving all those things we want or need to achieve.

Hold the belief that "I am in charge of my mind and therefore my results" and understand that, crucial to our overall success is the recognition that — sometimes the way our mind operates can be unhelpful to us and — we have control over our own mind and can "reprogramme" it accordingly.

We all have "voices in our heads", internal dialogues and conversations going on in our mind.

Sometimes these voices can say some pretty unhelpful things – we can hold beliefs and thoughts that can limit or stop us from doing things. These are what we call "limiting beliefs".

Henry Ford famously said *"If you believe you can or believe you cannot do something, either way you are likely to be right".*

It's true – by saying you "can't" do something you are already setting yourself up to not do it!

It's important to notice when the voices in your mind are talking, and then take control of these voices (as if we have a giant personal remote control in hand).

We can pause the voices, we can turn down the volume and, more importantly, we can "reprogramme" these voices.

We can reprogramme the limiting beliefs to something much more useful – we can presuppose something to be true and hold enabling beliefs that will enable us and help us to achieve things.

Enabling beliefs can be inspirational, powerful and motivational – they can help us "unlock" our thinking and be curious about a situation so we can get a different perspective.

We can hold a belief to be true in certain situations to help us and others – to enable us to move forward and achieve our objectives, goals and outcomes.

We can experiment with our own thinking and this can give us flexibility in our feelings and behaviours.

In situations where we feel stuck or confused, we can hold an enabling belief.

The following are just a handful of motivational enabling beliefs, two with corresponding narrative to their potential use and others for you to think about yourself – employing the strategy that Your Mind is Your Kingdom.

"If you always do what you've always done, you will always get what you've always got"

If something isn't working and you are doing the "same old thing" over and over again you will get the same result.

By doing something differently it might give you a different (and potentially *better*) result.

By seizing an opportunity to try things in a different way you are opening up all sorts of possibilities – and if you don't try things in a different way, how will you know what you are missing out on?

This is where knowledge sharing and networking comes into greatest effect.

You can learn from other administrative professionals by sharing knowledge and best practice.

In the interactive world of the world wide web, there are some amazing resources out there – all available at the touch of a button on your laptop or trusty "hand held". My daughter's favourite saying is "if you don't know something, Google it, mummy!"

Build up your own Resources List for inspirational sources of information and a catalyst for putting into practice this enabling belief.

"There is no such thing as failure, only feedback"

Many of you will have a formal appraisal process at your organisation. Recognise that feedback is crucial to your overall success and high quality feedback is given for your own career progression.

Those voices in our head may receive certain feedback with a response along the lines of "well, you failed there didn't you!". Sound familiar? This is not a particularly useful internal dialogue to have.

By holding the belief that "there is no such thing as failure, only feedback", this will open up more opportunities and possibilities for you to learn from feedback.

So, the project you've worked on may not have gone as well as you liked or hoped – so what can you learn from it?

Knowing what you now know, in hindsight, what could you have done differently?

If you were to run a similar project again, what could you do more of? Less of?

What will you replicate? What will you do the same? What will you do differently?

And here are some other enabling beliefs for you to think about – remembering that Your Mind Is Your Kingdom...

- "Choice is better than no choice."
- "If one person can do something then anyone can."

- "The person with the most flexibility in thinking and behaviour has the most influence over any interaction."
- "I am in charge of my mind and therefore my results."

The 'B' Pearl:

> *"The happiness of your life depends on the quality of your thoughts."*
> *Marcus Aurelius*

"Synchronised Fish and Chip Eating"   Few Peeps©

C is for Communication

C is for... Communication : VAK's amazing!

As an Executive PA you need to communicate with internal and external customers. Very quickly you need to get on someone else's wavelength in order to communicate effectively with them and create good rapport. You need to think about the best way to communicate in any given situation (face to face, email, text message, online/virtual meeting, telephone call...) then think about the language you will use to communicate.

People use terminology, phrases and words that relates to how they process their world and that's what I want to introduce in this Pearl of Wisdom.

We are all complex beings – with neurological pathways buzzing with activity, skilfully multi-tasking with organisational expertise and company knowledge at our fingertips... we are seeing, hearing, feeling, smelling and tasting our way to PA excellence and success!

But did you know that, whilst we access all five senses to "make sense" of our worlds, in fact most of us have a dominant or primary sense that we use over the others? That dominant sense can mean we favour certain words, phrases and vocabulary.

Being able to identify your own and others' dominant sense can be a useful thing to do to ensure you communicate as effectively as possible.

Take a few minutes to think back to the last meeting you were involved in and re-live the most memorable bits – collect the memories in your mind.

Then, think about how you remembered it: Did you create a visual picture of the events? Was it a "snapshot", a still image? Was it a "mini movie"? Was it in colour?

Or did you notice the sounds within the experience – people's voices, music or the natural sounds of the surroundings?

Or maybe the memory was about feelings inside – happiness (the meeting went really well!) or tension (the Sales Director and Managing Director could not agree on anything!).

Whichever one of these ways of reconstructing your memory was the first and/or most recognisable indicates your likely dominant sense – or your lead Representational System. Quite simply, it is how you create a "representation" or "re-present" your world – either in

- pictures (the Visuals – or The V),
- sounds (the Auditory – or The A), or
- feelings (the Kinaesthetics – or The K).

This is our VAK System – one that you as a PA can tap into to communicate really effectively with the people you work with.

An indicator of your Representation or VAK System is the language that you use – particular words and phrases that we call "Predicates".

The V

If you have a predominantly Visual Representational System then you're likely to use words and phrases like:

- "I see what you mean"
- "I get the picture"
- "Things are looking great"
- "We need to focus on this aspect."

And, because you can see in your "mind's eye" what you're talking about you're likely to use your arms and body to draw out in front of you the very thing you're describing! You will notice how things look around you – their shape, form and colour – the aesthetics.

The A

If you have a predominantly Auditory Representational System then you're likely to talk in predicates that are sound or music related, as examples:

- "We discussed the situation"
- "I'd like to listen to your ideas"
- "I do like the sound of that".

You might be great at tuning into new ideas.

The K

If you have a predominantly Kinaesthetic Representational System then you're likely to use language that is feelings, movement or touch related:

- "I'm under pressure"
- "I like the feeling of that"
- "Things are really moving now"

- "He's hot on quality control."

You probably have a pretty clear idea of where you experience your feelings too. If you're stressed you may touch your head, if you're hungry you may touch your stomach and for you to really optimise any learning, you probably want to be there, doing it as a first-hand experience.

So, why is this useful I hear you cry? "Tell me more" say the Auditory readers!

"I get a feeling this is really beneficial stuff – how can I take this great new learning and really get to grips with it in the office to communicate effectively?" ask the Kinaesthetic readers.

"So, that's great you've painted a picture of what this VAK thing is all about – can we look at it in relation to the Executive PA role?" the Visual readers request.

What is the use of my newfound knowledge?

Before I answer your question, let me ask you a couple of questions.

How often have you met someone for the first time and felt that you got along really well and immediately seemed to be on the "same wavelength"? And... how often have you met someone for the first time and found it really difficult to keep the conversation going?

The reason for this could be because you are either talking the same or a different "VAK Language".

If a primarily visual person is using all their visual type predicates, an auditory person is likely to "switch off".

However two "visual" people are much more likely to create quicker and deeper rapport and be "comfortable" with each other because they are, in effect, talking the same language.

So, next time you are listening to colleagues or friends in conversation, notice what words they tend to use and favour. Read through your emails in your inbox and notice any patterns of predicates favoured by those you work with. What Representational System do you think they are?

If you've discovered you are a primarily Visual Representation System and your manager is Auditory, in order to communicate effectively with him / her you can adjust your language and include more auditory predicates.

And that just leaves me to end this Pearl of Wisdom with a beautiful quote from Nelson Mandela:

The 'C' Pearl:

> *"If you speak to a man in a language he understands, that goes to his head.*
> *If you speak to him in his language that goes to his heart."*
> *Nelson Mandela*

"The Piggyback of True Love"   Few Peeps©

D is for Delegation

D is for...Delegation

Rarely does Delegation take the limelight – the starring role as an important "technique" for your overall success (and the overall success of your team). So in this Pearl of Wisdom (drum-roll please), I'd like to welcome to the stage: Delegation.

I've called Delegation a "technique". In my opinion, that is what it is and, as with any technique, it takes practice. Let's think about Delegation in terms of the following:

- What are the reasons people don't delegate?
- What's important about delegating?
- The "when" of delegation
- The "who" of delegation
- The "how" of delegation.

What are the reasons people don't delegate?

So, I put my hand up... here I am sharing my wisdom on delegation and I own up to the fact that, in the past, I haven't delegated because that little voice in my head is saying "I like doing things my way. I know how to do this – so it's easy just to do it myself rather than to take the time and effort to explain it all to someone else. Anyway they might not do it the same way as me – and, of course, my way is the best".

Sound familiar?! We need to understand that delegation is important.

So, what's important about delegation?

1. You can free up your time to develop skills in other areas, and
2. You can develop other people's skills and abilities.

So, there's another D word that skips hand-in-hand across the stage with Delegation.

Development

In essence, delegation allows you to make the best use of your time and skills and it helps other people in the team grow and develop to reach their full potential.

The "When" of Delegation

The power of questioning comes into being here! Ask yourself:

Is this a task that only I can do – or can someone else do it? (is confidential / sensitive information involved?)

Does the task provide an opportunity to grow and develop another person's skills?

Is this a recurring task?

By delegating now, will I be saving time in the long term?

Do I have enough time to delegate the task effectively? You need to think about the time involved in any training provision, questions and answers, opportunities to check progress and rework if necessary.

Keep thinking long-term. This might take some time and effort now. However, in the long-term you could be freeing up your time and ultimately aiding development.

The "Who" of Delegation

Think about the person you are delegating to.

What skills, knowledge and experience do they have in relation to the task?

Are they going to need training (and do you have the time and resources available to provide this)?

What do you know about the way this person likes to work?

How independent are they?

What do they want from their job?

What is their current workload like and do they have time to take on more work?

The "How" of Delegation

Firstly, as with any situation, you need to be really clear about your desired outcome – what is it you want or need to achieve?

Involve the person in the whole delegation process – discuss and decide with them what tasks are to be delegated.

Agree with them how this will work.

Should the person wait to be told what to do? Ask what to do? Recommend what should be done then act? Act and then report results immediately? Take action then report periodically?

Ensure you match responsibility with authority (remembering that ultimate accountability is with you).

Communication flow is key and you need to be available to answer questions.

Quieten that little voice in your head that says your way of completing a task is the best – someone else may complete the task differently to you.

We all have our own ways of working. Ensure you focus on the result.

Get the person to recommend solutions and problems (rather than simply providing the answer) and ensure you provide praise and recognition throughout.

Discuss timelines and deadlines and set aside time to review submitted work.

Get the balance right between giving enough space for people to use their abilities whilst still monitoring and supporting them to ensure the job is done effectively.

Only accept work you are satisfied with – if you accept work you are not satisfied with the team member will not learn to do the task properly.

Share the Belief that ***"There is no failure, only feedback"*** and that the best feedback is given for someone's development.

So, there we are. Delegation and Development have taken the limelight – our stars of the stage and I'm sure you'll join me in giving them the standing ovation they deserve.

The 'D' Pearl:

> *"One of life's greatest joys comes not from what you achieve in your life, it's what you inspire others to achieve in theirs."*
> *Nick Fewings*

"A Mother's Touch"   Few Peeps©

E is for Empathy

E is for... Empathy

Empathy (according to <u>www.diffen.com</u>) is *"the ability to mutually experience the thoughts, emotions, and direct experience of others".*

A useful thing to be able to do I'm sure you'd agree, particularly in your position as an Executive PA working with lots of different characters.

So what is the benefit of being empathetic and how can we best empathise with our managers and teams?

What is the benefit of being empathetic?

By empathising with someone, you are taking the time and effort to try to understand things from their point of view.

You are working with the fact that most of us like to be (and indeed want to be) valued and respected in the workplace.

We want people to take the time to understand things from our point of view.

By empathising with someone you are gaining more of an awareness of a situation – and that can open up choice, opportunities and flexibility around your own behaviours.

By empathising with someone and respecting and valuing them – they, in turn will respect and value you. And that sets a pretty solid foundation for a great working relationship, I'm sure you'd agree.

How can we best empathise with our managers and teams?

When empathising face to face with our managers and teams, use the research of former Harvard Professor Albert Mehrabian. As a reminder from the A is for Assertiveness Pearl of Wisdom, communication can be broken down into three elements (the 3Vs), namely:

1. Verbal – the words that we speak,
2. Vocal – the tone that we use, and
3. Visual – the body language that we display.

To empathise with someone match their Verbal, Vocal and Visual communication. By taking on the physiology of someone else you will more easily be able to identify with what they are experiencing.

Think about what you already know about the person you want to empathise with. What's important to them? See, hear and feel the world from their perspective.

Put the person you are empathising with at the forefront of the conversation. Be precise in the language that you use. Say things like:

- "I appreciate your point of view and… "
- "I can see / hear where you're coming from and… "
- "I get your perspective and… "
- "It's obvious to me that you're really passionate / upset / frustrated / excited with this… "
- "I understand how you are feeling… "

Sound back and repeat particular words or phrases that they have used. A person's vocabulary, the terms and words they use are "precious" to them – they mean something to them (which could be different to your own interpretation).

Keep gentle eye contact. Let the person finish saying what they want to say. Regular nods of your head will indicate you are listening and value what they are sharing with you.

And then, ask that one Great Question – "what do you need from me?".

The 'E' Pearl:

> *"The great gift of human beings is that we have the power of empathy."*
> *Meryl Streep*

"I will"   Few Peeps©

F is for Feedback

F is for... Feedback-to-self & Focus (not Flibbertigibbet)

I really do like the sound of that word: Flibbertigibbet.

It's eccentric and flighty and has an onomatopoeic quality.

However, I most certainly do not like it when I become that word – a flibbertigibbet flitting from one thing to the next, a bit of this, a bit of that (without completing or achieving anything in full!).

I know when it happens too... when my "to do" list extends to more than one A4 page, when my inbox is full of unopened and unread messages, when I have deadlines to meet, when I glance at my watch and see that I'm "running out of time"... then.

My flitting, scatter-brained and unfocused flibbertigibbet self is far from productive.

For me, this is a prime "Feedback-to-Self and Focus" moment.

My first bit of Feedback-to-Self is "well done"! Well done for recognising that this is what is happening (and for being honest with myself!). Having awareness of what's going on in a situation – what's happening for you – is a Great Thing. Because once you have awareness you can then take ownership of the situation and you have choice and opportunity available to you to change the situation (for the better of course!). So with awareness comes opportunity. And with opportunity comes change.

A great model to use for Feedback-to-Self and Focus is the ABC model (which you'll recognise from the A is for Assertiveness Pearl of Wisdom), the basis of which lies in asking great questions of yourself (and answering them honestly!)

A – Antagonist

What specifically is it that has happened to make me feel or behave his way?

What can I do to eliminate or change this Antagonist in the future?

(and remember the belief "if you can't change something, change the way you think about it"!)

B – Behaviour

What behaviour am I exhibiting? And how helpful is this behaviour?

What could I be doing more of?

What could I be focusing more on?

What could I be doing less of?

What could I be focusing less on?

What could I stop doing?

What could I stop focusing on?

What could I start doing?

What could I start focusing on?

What could I continue doing?

What could I continue focusing on?

What have I done in the past that has worked in a similar situation?

What have I focused on in the past that has worked in a similar situation?

What resources do I have available to me?

What do I need to Focus on that is Urgent?

What do I need to Focus on that is Important? (Thank you, Stephen Covey!)

What do I need right now?

C – Consequence

What is it I want (or need) to achieve?

What is the consequence of my current behaviour? And how useful is this consequence?

What would a better consequence be?

What do I want (or need) the consequence to be?

The 'F' Pearl:

> *"If we did all the things we are capable of, we would literally astound ourselves."*
> *Thomas Edison*

"Checking you're on the list"   Few Peeps©

G is for Gateway

G is for... Gateway

As a PA and Administrative Professional, what other titles can you relate to?

Gateway, Confidante,

Peace Maker, Juggler,

Mind Mapper, Networker,

Time keeper, Trainer.

Fortune Teller, Lion Tamer,

Dictionary, Thesaurus,

Mind Reader, Zoo Keeper

Mentor, Minute Taker.

Proof Reader, Typist,

Coach, Decision Maker,

Trouble-shooter, Acrobat,

Strategist, Negotiator.

Right Hand, Left Hand,

Team Motivator,

Travel Booker, Budgeter,

Events Co-ordinator.

The 'G' Pearl:

> *"What you allow is what will continue." Anonymous*

" All because he does not want wet feet"   Few Peeps©

H is for Helpful

H is for... Helpful

When I ask my clients for a skill and attribute beginning with "H", "Helpful" always appears top of the list and that's understandable. It's understandable because the very nature of the role of an Executive PA is one of assisting and helping others out to ensure the manager(s), office and organisation are operating as smoothly as possible.

I know. I've been there. As a former EA working for a team of attorneys in a busy legal department in the USA I was "helpful" personified. I also kept an objective view that being helpful doesn't necessarily mean we say "yes" all the time.

We are not being helpful to ourselves, our sanity and wellbeing if we always say "yes". We need to be really clear about where our work priorities lie – what the boundaries of our role are in order that we concentrate our time and energy on the right things.

It's okay to say "no" and that, in itself, is an art form.

Helpful ways to say "no" (without actually saying the word "no"!)

Use the "no" that fits best with your situation.

As general guidance, remember someone has probably asked you to help them because they believe you are capable and able to do it. Thank them for asking you. Help the other person understand your point of view and perspective by saying "I'm sure you will appreciate... ".

1. The "Final Word" no

"Thank you for asking me. I would prefer not to do this. As I'm sure you will appreciate I have a deadline to meet for preparation of the management meeting packs."

2. The Rescheduling No

"Whilst I can't do it now – I could certainly help you later".

Make sure you keep your promise to the person you have agreed to help out. Make a diary note or set a reminder. This will maintain your credibility and professionalism in the workplace.

3. The Problem Solving No

"I'm not in a position to help you, have you considered phoning technical support?"

Suggest an alternative solution to the person asking for your help. We've all worked for the manager who states "Come to me with solutions, not problems" and this "no" satisfies this practice.

4. The Negotiating No

"If I help you with x, then I would really appreciate your help with y. Is that okay?"

Get the others person's agreement to this negotiation. This is a great opportunity to help each other out by tapping in to each other's expertise, skills and love for doing a particular aspect of work.

5. The Reprioritising No

"I'm happy to do this, however I'll have to reprioritise my workload a bit. What would you suggest?"

6. The "One Last Time" No

"I know I've helped you in the past and I'll help you again this time. As I'm sure you will appreciate, with my demanding workload my priorities need to be with xxxxx so from now on could I suggest you ask technical support / follow the printed procedures I've produced. Is that okay?"

Get the other person's agreement to this suggestion. In some situations you can produce an "operators manual" or typed instructions / procedures that can easily be followed without interrupting your time and which will ensure the other person can do this themselves ongoing.

The 'H' Pearl:

> *"Be a fence jumper*
> *instead of a fence sitter."*
> *Robert V Taylor*

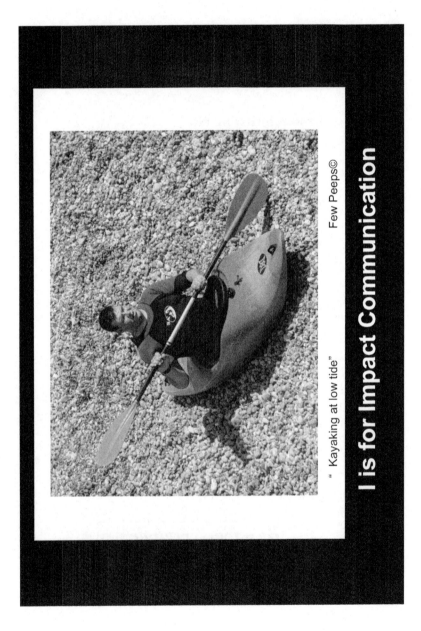

" Kayaking at low tide"

Few Peeps©

I is for Impact Communication

I is for... IMPACT Communication

To create an IMPACT when communicating you need to be aware of the 3Vs research of Mehrabian (you can read more about this in the A is for Assertiveness Pearl of Wisdom).

Think about how you're going to use the Vocal element and Visual element to add the IMPACT you need and want.

When considering the Verbal element, you can apply a simple yet highly effective IMPACT model to formulate your wording and incorporate "The Power of Three".

The Power of Three

"The Power of Three" is a principle that implies that things that come in threes are more satisfying, effective and memorable. It's fun, thought-provoking and, more importantly, when applied, can add real impact to your communication.

The Good, The Bad and The Ugly

Think about it. When you introduce three things – this is the smallest number you can use to produce a rhythm or pattern to your communication, whilst still remaining catchy, simple and memorable. All Good then (not Bad or Ugly).

You'll notice the use of the Power of Three in storytelling, films and advertising.

Think back to your favourite childhood books – "Goldilocks and the Three Bears", "The Three Billy Goats Gruff" or "The Three Little Pigs" (excuse me whilst I have a flashback to my Ladybird book collection!).

Cuddled up on the sofa watching a movie you might choose "The Three Stooges", "Three Amigos" or "Three Men and a Baby". Or, during the festive season you might settle down to watch a Dickensian classic such as "A Christmas Carol" (not the Muppet version please!) where Scrooge is visited by the Ghosts of Christmas Past, Present and Future.

Traditionally, sporting events award Gold, Silver and Bronze to worthy winners. Famous advertising slogan examples are the UK's "Stop, Look and Listen" campaign to promote safety when crossing our busy roads. How about "A Mars a day helps you work, rest and play"?

Even hashtags are joining in the fun with one of my favourites being #ThisGirlCan, the Sport England campaign inspiring more women to be active.

Three priests and three boys appear in Mozart's 1791 Opera "The Magic Flute".

The Holy Trinity is the father, the son and the Holy Spirit.

On the witness stand your oath is to "tell the truth, the whole truth and nothing but the truth".

Some of the most famous and memorable speeches practice "The Power of Three".

In Martin Luther King Jr's "Non-Violence and Racial Justice" speech he compares "insult, injustice and exploitation" with "justice, goodwill and brotherhood". And an example of the attraction of "The Power of Three" is evident when we quote "blood, sweat and tears" – an amendment to Winston Churchill's original "blood, toil, tears and sweat" (which appears on a five-pound note!).

By including the principles of The Power of Three in your own communication (whether written or verbal) your audience is more likely to remember what you have shared.

The IMPACT Model

The IMPACT Model is a perfect format for putting forward your ideas, proposals and suggestions. It's like a "mini-business-case" and incorporates The Power of Three to add memorability. Here's the Model:

I = Introduce your idea/proposal and employ KISS (Keep It Short and Simple)

M = Main Reasons: identify the main reasons and use the "Power of Three"

P = Problems: Be ready to answer any potential problems or queries that could arise

A = Appeal: to Logic (e.g. it will save us money) and Appeal to Emotion (e.g. it is good for team morale)

C = Credibility – add this with supporting evidence, statistics and/or information

T = Thank your audience for listening and take any questions.

And here are two examples of IMPACT Communication:

Example One

I =   *I suggest you put into practice "The Power of Three" when communicating.*

M =   *You will be able to share knowledge that is 1) more effective, 2) impactful and 3) memorable.*

P =   *I agree it might take some practice, but "practice makes perfect".*

A =   *By using "The Power of Three" you can better engage, inspire and lead those you are communicating with.*

C =   *Think about some of our famous orators such as Martin Luther King Jr and Winston Churchill.*

T =   *Thanks for taking the time to let me share my suggestion with you. Do you have any questions?*

Example Two

I =   *I suggest you book on a Your Excellency training course.*

M =   *The training has been specially designed for the EA and PA Professional and the learning is 1) current 2) relevant and 3) instantly-useable.*

P =   *You think it might be expensive? Your Excellency pride themselves on remaining competitive on price and can help you if you have to self-fund too.*

A =   *So their training is cost-effective and will provide you with the skills and confidence you need to be truly exceptional.*

C =   *They have a Learner Success Stories page on their website with some fantastic video comments from graduates and learners.*

T =   *Thanks for listening and do you have any questions?*

The 'I' Pearl:

> **Your privileged position as a PA means you see, hear and experience what's happening in your organisation from the "shop floor" to the Board Room Table.**
>
> **You're ideally placed then to put forward your ideas, proposals and suggestions.**
>
> **Make sure you do this with IMPACT!**
>
> **Lindsay Taylor**

"In the heat of the moment"   Few Peeps©

J is for Juggling

J is for... Juggling the demands of more than one Executive

Many PAs are in roles where they are supporting more than one Executive, having to juggle their time efficiently and effectively, and remain calm under pressure.

The key to successful management of the demands of more than one Executive comes down to great communication – with those you are supporting and with yourself!

Here is a list of useful techniques to help you successfully work with multiple demands:

- Speak to each of your Executives individually to ensure they are aware of your workload and the fact that you are assisting other people.

  At the same time, assure them that you appreciate that their demands are important.

  Share with them the fact that you want to be as effective and efficient as possible.

  Ultimately you are all working towards the same goal of a smooth working relationship.

- Become familiar with the preferred workings of each team member – people work and 'tick' in different ways, and each Executive may have different expectations of you.

You know which Executive is happy with you writing up a report and circulating it without them even looking over it for final approval.

Likewise, you know the Executive who will want to tweak that report (for the fifth time!) before it gets circulated.

- Verbally repeat your Executive's demands to them to ensure you have understood their request correctly.

Never assume anything!

- Always ensure you know the deadline for a task, project or request so you can prioritise tasks and demands accordingly.

Give yourself more "breathing space" by asking "When is the *absolute latest* you need this by?"

In theory, it's great to have a prioritised work list for the day (or week) ahead.

However, in practice, we know that this list will constantly change – just as soon as you've put together a prioritised list, one of your Executives will appear with a mini-emergency that needs your assistance!

You need to be able to re-jig the list and be flexible in your approach.

- If you are lucky enough to have others who can help you in the office, delegate some of your workload.

For more on delegation read the D is for Delegation Pearl of Wisdom.

- When you have completed a project or demand, ask your Executive for feedback.

  What would they have done differently?

  More of?

  Less of?

  Remember that good feedback is given to help your personal development and you have a choice what to do with this feedback!

- If a project or task didn't quite live up to your expectations, hold the belief that *"there is no failure, only feedback"*.

  Ask yourself: "what would I have done differently knowing what I know now?"

  And "how can I learn from this experience for the future?"

- Remember: you are one person with two hands – there is a limit to the tasks that you can fit into a working day.

  Be realistic with your own expectations for working your way through that prioritised list.

  Be prepared to say "no" if you can't meet a demand or request – saying "no" and providing alternative suggestions is a skill in its own right.

  You can read more about the different ways to say "no" in the H is for Helpful Pearl of Wisdom.

- Take inspiration from Mary Poppins! While watching this all-time classic film with my daughter I took inspiration from Mary Poppins, before she burst into song:

> *"In every job that must be done,*
>
> *There is an element of fun.*
>
> *You find the fun, and snap!*
>
> *The job's a game.*
>
> *And every task you undertake*
>
> *Becomes a piece of cake,*
>
> *A lark, a spree,*
>
> *It's very clear to see*
>
> *That a spoonful of sugar helps the medicine go down."*

Hold the thought that, if you approach a task or demand in the right frame of mind, with a treat/motivator that is your "spoonful of sugar", it can, and will, become "a piece of cake"!

There is a great saying by Henry Ford that:

> **"If you believe you can or believe you cannot do something, either way you are likely to be right".**

Approach all tasks in a "can do" mind-set and you are well on the way to achieving great things and being able to juggle those demands.

The 'J' Pearl:

> *"Our success is not just defined by what we know.*
> *More importantly it is down to the strength of the relationships we build with others."*
> *Nick Fewings*

"Two stop or not two stop, that is the question"   Few Peeps©

K is for KISS

K is for... KISS

KISS is an acronym for Keep It Short & Simple.

This is an effective strategy that can be used to ensure the best impact when communicating.

We all have different amounts of information that we like to process and work with.

Some people like lots of detail.

Their sentence structure is long and contains lots of "ands" – and just when you think they've finished talking and telling you what they want to say... they will add something else!

They relish having to scroll down on an email and pick up on the detail.

Other people are more "big picture".

They just want to work with a general overview or aim and don't want to get caught up in the "nitty gritty" details.

Their sentence structure is shorter (and could give the impression that they are being curt or rude).

Put a detail person and big picture person together and this is when it gets interesting.

The detail individual will be craving more detail from the big picture individual.

The big picture individual may "switch off" (ever noticed someone's eyes glazing over?!) as the detail person shares too much detail with them.

The big picture individual may well miss crucial information or requests of them in their glazed over state!

As a strategy then, it is good practice to seal things with a KISS. Keep It Short and Simple.

Say what you want to say in one succinct, impactful sentence so you engage your entire audience – big picture and detail alike.

When writing emails requesting information or a response:

Ensure the request is put at the beginning of the email (so the big picture preference is more likely to read it).

Then you can back up your email with "and for those who would like more detail... " to satisfy the detail preference who wants to scroll down!

And of course, in your busy world as an Executive PA and Office Professional you will also be saving yourself valuable time and energy by using KISS.

The 'K' Pearl:

> *"If you can't explain it to a six year old, you don't understand it yourself."*
> *Albert Einstein*

"O yay, o yay, o yay"   Few Peeps©

L is for Listening

L is for... Listening with your whole body

Listening is the key to creating and maintaining rapport and the great working relationship that we all want with our Executive(s) and team members.

Listening is a skill and for many of us, it is a skill we can improve on.

The crème de la crème of listening involves listening with your whole body and then mirroring or matching the person you are listening to in order to create and maintain rapport, based on the popular saying that "people like people who are like themselves".

Once we have great rapport with someone, we are then more easily able to influence or persuade them – with integrity of course – so that we can achieve our goals and outcomes. The "integrity" element here is of utmost importance when influencing – we need to ensure the person we are influencing is being taken to a good place as well as ourselves in achieving our goals and outcomes.

Let's use Mehrabian's research introduced in the "A is for Assertiveness" Pearl of Wisdom as a basis for putting this "whole body listening" into practice.

Based on the research of former Harvard Professor Albert Mehrabian, communication can be broken down into the 3Vs, namely:

1) Verbal – the words that we speak

2) Vocal – the tone that we use, and

3) Visual – the body language that we display.

Listen with your ears to the Verbal element:

We all have a preference for phrases, terminology and favourite sayings. Our own personal interpretation of vocabulary may be very different to someone else's.

Notice what specific words and phrases the person you are listening to has used. Pick out particular phrases and words to repeat back when talking to them.

Based on the popular saying "people like people who are like themselves", by using the same "language" and words as the person you are listening to this demonstrates your respect for what they are saying.

You are keeping the conversation "clean" by using their language without "dirtying" the conversation with your own preferences. This accounts for a lot in creating and maintaining great rapport.

Listen with your ears to the Vocal element:

Listen to how someone is using their voice and vocal chords. What tone of voice are they using? What emphasis are they placing on words with the intonation of their voice? How fast or slow are they speaking? What volume are they using? What does this tell you?

Listen with your eyes to the Visual element:

Based on Mehrabian's research we know that 55% of communication comes down to the Visual element – how we deliver our message. As a listener then, we can assess a lot from noticing what is happening in a person's body language including their physiology (facial expressions), gestures and movement. What can you see happening? We can listen with our eyes and use this information to be curious about what is going on for that person.

The 'L' Pearl:

> *"The word 'listen'*
> *contains the same letters*
> *as the word 'silent'."*
> *Alfred Brendel*

" Lazing on a sunny afternoon"

Few Peeps©

M is for Manage your Energy

M is for... Manage your Energy

One of the most popular training sessions I deliver is on the topic of managing your energy.

The learning I share is based on an article in the Harvard Business Review by Tony Schwartz and Catherine McCarthy (October 2007).

The article introduces two facts, namely:

1.   time is a limited resource, and
2.   personal energy is renewable.

This resonates with me and I hope with you too.

It makes absolute sense that we can replenish our own energy and in doing so build up our resilience in terms of our physical, emotional and mental wellbeing.

We need to recognise what behaviours are draining us of energy and take responsibility for changing them.

We need to incorporate more of the things that will replenish our energy.

Then and only then will we be able to "recharge" ourselves.

The changes that we can put into place are labelled as "rituals" by Schwartz & McCarthy.

These are behaviours that can initially be practiced intentionally (preferably at designated times of the day) with the goal of them becoming a habit and unconscious activities.

Our personal energy can be divided into four dimensions – physical, emotional, mental and spiritual.

For each dimension, we can practice rituals that will ensure we are replenishing our personal energy.

Physical Energy

- "Eat little and often".
  Eating smaller meals/snacks every three hours will sustain our energy levels.
- Take a break away from your desk – every 90 or 120 minutes.
  Even if the break is only for several minutes, it means you have disengaged from work and will return renewed and energised.
- Set a slightly earlier bedtime.
  Our bodies need a regular dose of 7 to 8 hours of sleep otherwise we're likely to wake up feeling tired.
- Make sure you engage in some form of exercise. (Schwartz & McCarthy recommend cardiovascular training at least 3 times a week and strength training at least once a week).

Emotional Energy

We all recognise that we are more energised when we have positive thoughts and emotions. Unfortunately, human nature is such that we can't sustain positive thoughts 24/7.

When faced with the challenges and demands of our busy role, we revert to our innate human "fight or flight" response.

This can drain us of energy and impact our logical and reasonable thinking.

We need a better awareness of how and when we are feeling different emotions throughout the working day so that we can take better control of these emotions and in doing so improve the quality of our energy.

Build on positive emotions by expressing appreciation to others – this has benefits to the giver and the receiver.

Set aside regular times to do this and think about different ways of expressing your appreciation (email, phone call, conversation, a lunch or dinner).

Rather than playing the victim and blaming other people or circumstances for your problems, change your story.

Recognise that you have a choice about how you view situations, and there is a direct correlation between your story and the emotions you feel.

Use different "lenses" to expand your perspective and understanding of a challenging situation. Use the 1) Reverse Lens, 2) Long Lens and 3) Wide Lens to intentionally cultivate more positive emotions.

1. With the *reverse lens*, consider the situation from another's perspective. Ask yourself "What would the other person in this conflict say and in what ways might that be true?"
2. With the *long lens* ask, "How will I most likely view this situation in six months?"

3. With the *wide lens* ask, "Regardless of the outcome of this issue, how can I grow and learn from it?"

Mental Energy

- Identify what things distract you and affect your concentration.
  If you know you need to remain focused on a task, move yourself away from distractions.
- At the end of your working day identify the most important challenge for the next day.
  Make this a priority when you arrive into work the next morning.
- Batch similar tasks together.
  Complete them at designated times during your day.
- Turn off those email notification "pop ups"!

Spiritual Energy

- Identify activities that make you feel happy and fulfilled.
  What makes you come alive?
  Do more of these.
- Identify what's important to you (this is my optimum coaching question) and allocate your time and energy to these things.
- Identify what you value and then live up to those values – "practice what you preach".

The 'M' Pearl:

> *"It's not selfish to love yourself, take care of yourself and to make your happiness a priority.*
> *It's necessary."*
> *Anonymous*

" Contemplating life "

Few Peeps©

N is for Neuro Linguistic Programming

N is for... Neuro Linguistic Programming

Many of you know that I specialise in delivering training to EAs and PAs across the world and that I am a former PA myself.

What you may not know is that I am a Practitioner in NLP – Neuro Linguistic Programming – and I'd love to share with you a bit more about this fascinating subject...

Admittedly Neuro Linguistic Programming sounds very "jargonny" doesn't it?

Its abbreviation NLP looks a bit more friendly – but many of you may still be outwardly cringing and frowning whilst reading this – *"urgh – sounds complicated to me... should I carry on reading this Pearl of Wisdom?"* Please do.

"Complicated" was in fact my reaction when I first heard of NLP – but I was curious (which interestingly enough is the very foundation to all NLP learning).

NLP seemed to be popping up in conversation everywhere and I wanted to know what all the hype was about.

The more I found out, the more I became interested – so much so that I trained to be a Practitioner in NLP.

Where did NLP start?

NLP was born in the 1970s at the University of Santa Cruz, California.

Richard Bandler, an Information Sciences student and Dr John Grinder, a Professor of Linguistics, studied people they considered to be excellent communicators and agents of change.

From these early days, NLP has developed around the modelling of excellence and understanding *"the difference that makes the difference"*.

The tools and techniques have been refined into simple, user-friendly formats that can be applied to everyday life.

The main principles are around understanding behaviour patterns of ourselves and others thereby developing flexibility in order to achieve what we really want.

Nowadays, NLP is widely used by leading edge businesses to develop competitive advantage and manage change.

Additionally, individuals are utilising NLP techniques for personal development inside and outside of their work environment.

Whilst training to be an NLP Practitioner I thought *"wow – if only I'd had some of these skills and awareness during my working life as a PA, because this NLP stuff is really good and so relevant to the admin professional who is working with different (and sometimes hard to understand!) personalities"*.

What is it?

There are lots of definitions of NLP – here are a few:

- "The art and science of personal excellence"
- "The study of subjective experience"
- "It's what makes you and other people tick"
- "A toolkit for personal and organisational change"
- "Influencing others with integrity"
- "Helping people make sense of their reality."

My personal favourite is *"It's what makes you and other people tick"* because this is a jargon-free easy-to-understand definition that really sums NLP up in a nutshell.

The easiest way to understand NLP is to break down the N, L and P :

- **Neuro** is the use of our senses to filter and process our experiences.
  We see, hear, feel, taste and smell our own version of reality.
- **Linguistic** is the language we use to express our interpretation of reality.
- **Programming** is the patterns of behaviour and thinking that we follow as a result of our filtering and processing of experiences.
  These patterns create structure to our experiences from which we communicate.
  Once we recognise our own structures and patterns we can change them to influence our outcomes.
  Similarly when we understand structures and patterns of others we can influence and

support them, thereby creating a world of possibilities.

In summary, NLP is devoted to learning how to think and communicate with yourself and others more effectively.

The Model

The core principles or pillars of NLP are:

- **Rapport** – this is about relationship with yourself.
  It's about having congruence and integrity whereby the whole of you is in alignment.
  It's about relationships with others in order to effectively influence and achieve what you really want.

- **Sensory Awareness** – this is the "neuro" of neuro linguistic programming which means using your senses – looking at, listening to and feeling what is happening to you and others.

- **Outcome Thinking** – this is establishing exactly what you want.
  This could be what you want in any given situation or a larger life outcome.

- **Behavioural Flexibility** – this is about using choice to do or think differently when what you currently do is not working.
  This is essential in achieving your outcome.

Pillars of NLP

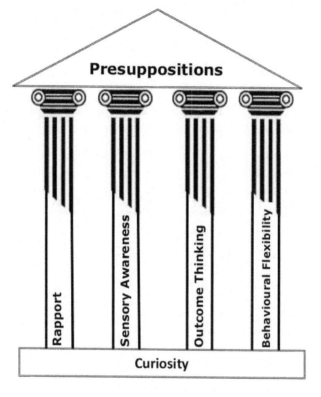

- **Curiosity** – this forms the foundations of the model.

  It is about accepting that you don't know all the answers but you are willing to use curiosity to investigate and understand what is happening within each of the four pillars.

  It is about questioning and noticing what you notice.

- **Presuppositions** – these are about freeing the beliefs and values that you hold.
  In conjunction with a non-judgmental curiosity, presuppositions can expand learning and awareness.

Why is NLP useful?

Imagine having the skills to know what it is you really want and you have all of the communication, awareness and flexibility to achieve it every time.

From the Model derives a multitude of tools and techniques that can be utilised to give you exactly that.

These tools and techniques become a way of life in your personal and professional environments and will help you establish and achieve your goals and directions.

As an Executive PA, NLP provides you with an awareness of how you "tick" and how others "tick" – particularly the people you support in your role.

With NLP skills and awareness, you can be flexible in your thinking and behaviour in order to get the response or reaction that you need.

You will have the skills to create deep rapport with those around you, to better understand where a person is "coming from".

The 'N' Pearl:

> *"You have brains in your*
> *head.*
> *You have feet in your*
> *shoes.*
> *You can steer yourself*
> *any direction you*
> *choose."*
> *Dr Seuss*

"Now this is how it feels"   Few Peeps©

O is for Opinionated

O is for...Opinionated

Opinionated? That's a matter of opinion!

Putting forward your Opinion with Impact

When you feel very strongly about something it can be easy to let your emotions get the better of you and by doing so you can lose or dilute the impact of sharing your opinion.

There's an art to putting forward and sharing your opinion in a way that "lands" with the best impact. Notice I've used the word "share" here – this is about *sharing* your opinion, not *enforcing* your opinion on someone else – it's about respecting the fact that not everyone will have the same opinion as you.

The following guidelines will help you put forward your opinion with impact.

1. Breathe! When you feel strongly about something this may show in your fast-paced breathing, body language and pace of talking. You need to get the balance right here between sharing your opinion with "passion" without appearing flustered, harassed or "bulldozing". By focusing on maintaining even, steady breathing this will help enormously.

2. Ground yourself and be assertive! Plant your feet firmly on the ground and ensure your body language is assertive – so match the level of someone else (if they are standing, you

stand, if they are sitting, you sit). Open the palms of your hands and maintain a steady, gentle eye-contact with the person you are talking to. Your tone of voice needs to be assertive too with an even paced steady rhythm that emphasises the important words or phrases at a volume that is audible to your audience (without shouting). *You can read more about assertiveness in the A is for Assertiveness Pearl of Wisdom.*

3. Favour Curiosity over Judgment. Human nature is such that we tend to "pre-judge" others based on our own experience and beliefs – put aside any prejudgments you make and instead be curious. Curiosity is the foundation to all learning and opens our mind to ensure we are more receptive and aware in any situation.

4. Acknowledge someone else's opinion. Not everyone will have the same opinion as you. We are all unique human beings with individual experiences, beliefs, upbringing, knowledge and learning. Acknowledge that someone else may have a different opinion to you, e.g. "I understand you have/may have a different opinion here and I'm sure, like me, you appreciate that we're all different."

5. Seal it with a KISS! (Keep It Short & Simple). Cut through any jargon by using simple language that can be instantly understood. *You can read more about this in the K is for KISS Pearl of Wisdom.*

6. Explain your reasons for having the opinion that you do: e.g. "This is my opinion because in my experience x has happened... " or "I'm basing my opinion on ... ."

7. Tailor your language to suit the person you are delivering your message to – learn about VAK systems. Did you know that, whilst we access all five senses to "make sense" of our worlds, in fact most of us have a dominant or primary sense that we use over the others? And the language and favoured vocabulary that we use relates directly to that primary sense. Talking someone else's language means you are more easily able to create rapport with them and have a "connection" – crucial if you want to deliver your message with real impact. *You can read more about this in the C is for Communication Pearl of Wisdom.*

As we've seen, Nelson Mandela said *"if you talk to a man in a language he understands that goes to his head. If you talk to him in his language, that goes to his heart".* In order to create deep rapport and deliver your message with real impact, you want to be able to use another person's preferred language set.

8. Be open to hearing someone else's opinion. Someone else has given you their time to listen to your opinion – which you've delivered with impact. Reciprocate by giving them time to share theirs.

The 'O' Pearl:

> ## "Tact is the art of making a point without making an enemy."
> ### Isaac Newton

"Snapping the snapper"   Few Peeps©

P is for Perceptual Positions

P is for... Perceptual Positions (step into my shoes...)

"The person with the most flexibility in thinking and behaviour has the most influence over any situation."

How often have you been in a situation and found yourself confused or frustrated at the response or behaviour of someone else?

How often have you asked yourself – *"why have they acted in such a defensive / negative / destructive / inappropriate way?"*

In situations where you are faced with confusion and frustration at someone else's attitude, behaviour or actions, what can you do?

Well, firstly you can have Curiosity, something I consider to be the foundation to all learning.

You need to have the curiosity to find out the reasons behind someone eliciting a particular behaviour or responded in the way that they have.

Because, without curiosity you can lose sight of what your original outcome for a situation is.

Then you can put into practice the technique known as "perceptual positions", which allows you to gain insight into a situation by looking at it and considering it from three different perspectives.

First Position (your own)

"Wearing your own shoes" and fully experiencing what is important to you. This is known as being "associated" into your experience.

Second Position (the other person's)

By "wearing their shoes" and being fully associated with what is important to them.

Third Position (from the outside)

By taking a disassociated and analytical view of what is happening between 1 and 2.

By gaining this insight we give ourselves choices and flexibility about the actions we can take in order to support our outcomes.

Here is the Technique:-

1. From first position and "in your own shoes" think about the situation from your point of view.
2. Ask yourself:
    What is important to me?
    How does this affect me?
    What is my desired outcome from this situation?
    Take a mental note of these.
3. From second position and stepping into "the other person's shoes", think about what is important to them.
4. See, hear and feel the world from their position.
5. Take on the other person's physiology and think about their beliefs and values, what do you already

know about this person that will help you understand it from their perspective?

This will allow you to become fully associated into their world.

6. From third position and like "a fly on the wall", you move to the position of an independent eye-witness.

   You observe and comment on the facts of the situation without feeling or emotion.

   You can therefore give yourself disassociated advice on what would be useful in order to improve the situation and gain a better understanding of what is going on.

A good way to work with this technique is to physically move between positions to experience the different perspectives.

Position two chairs – sit on one to experience first position then move to the other chair to experience second position. Stand back to experience third position from a distance.

Think about what happens when someone becomes "stuck" in any of the three positions too.

- A person stuck in first position can become selfish and egotistical.

- In second position the person can be over-influenced and co-dependent on the views of those around them.

- In third position a person can become emotionally-detached and unfeeling.

With the flexibility to move (physically and in your mind and thinking) you will find this technique beneficial to increase your awareness during a given situation.

And, of course, the person with the most flexibility in thinking and behaviour, has the most influence over any situation.

Perceptual Positions

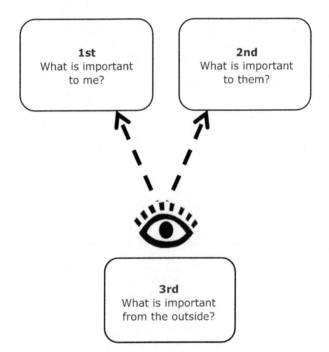

The 'P' Pearl:

> *"Sometimes we need to take a different perspective to see things clearly."*
> *Nick Fewings*

"Where are we?"   Few Peeps©

Q is for Quality Questions

Q is for...Quality Questions

"A Quality Question is made up of asking the right person the right question in the right way" Lindsay Taylor

Quality Questions give quality responses and answers. They provide you with the information you need or want quickly and efficiently. Ensuring you get it right first time will save you time and energy and will ensure your credibility in the workplace as a highly organised and time-efficient PA.

Firstly, ensure you are clear about the information you need or want and identify the best (and therefore right) person to get this information from.

What do you know about this person with regard to how they like to communicate (think about VAK systems and read the C is for Communication Pearl of Wisdom)?

Asking your question in the right way using a combination of their preferred language will ensure great rapport between you – and therefore a better likelihood of getting the very best (and highest quality) response.

Also think about whether it is going to be best / quicker to get the response you need by asking the question of someone face to face (or over the phone) or by sending the question via email?

Identify the right question to ask. Do you need to ask an "open question" to facilitate lots of information? Or do you need to clarify information or a request of you by asking a closed question (one that invites a yes or no response)?

I have a favourite open questions model that I introduce to PA clients (and one that raised a lot of giggling from my daughter when she was younger and believed "bottom" to be a rude word!). This is the "5 bottoms on a rugby post" model.

Transpose the word "bottoms" for "derrieres" or "behinds" – whichever you prefer – and I challenge you not to giggle like my daughter!

Imagine some rugby posts (the letter "H" for our "How" questions) and on the crossbar of the rugby posts imagine 5 rugby bottoms (or "W's" for our "W" questions – namely, What, Why, Where, Who, When).

You will notice that the "Why" question in the model has a warning triangle by it – the reason? Because asking a "why" question can be received in an accusatory way and therefore the response you get may be a defensive one.

Also, as a questioner you can find yourself in a "why" spiral, asking a quick succession of "why" questions whilst never quite getting the highest quality response.

Rephrasing your question to "what's important... " or "what's important about... " ensures you are getting to the real "crux" of a matter, the heart of the question and ensuring a quality response that has invited the respondent to think deeply about the question posed to them.

Open Questions

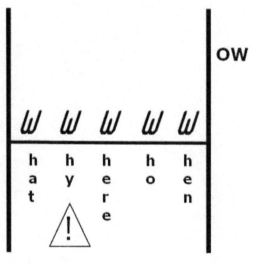

⚠ = What's important about....

The 'Q' Pearl:

> *"The art and science of asking questions is the source of all knowledge."*
> *Thomas Berger*

"Ready for the off"   Few Peeps©

R is for Red lorry, yellow lorry

R is for... Red lorry, yellow lorry

As a busy PA and Executive Assistant having to "think on your feet" is part and parcel of your role – you need to work quickly and efficiently without getting tongue-tied – in order to foster credibility and respect in your workplace.

So, how do you achieve this?

1. **"Failing to plan is planning to fail"**

   Be as prepared as you can be for every eventuality.

   Pre-empt any impending or likely situations that could arise, holding the belief that "Failing to plan is planning to fail."

   An excellent PA is proactive and always at least one step ahead of the situation.

2. **Identify your outcome – what do you want or need to achieve?**

   Once you've identified any impending or likely situations, articulate your outcome and what it is you need or want to achieve.

   Use precise, towards language to verbalise this outcome.

Towards language is vocabulary that has momentum and forward movement – you are moving towards achieving, gaining and getting the outcome you want.

Use the following format: [In the event that xxx happens, I will xxx.]

3. See, hear and feel it!

Rehearse the situation in your mind.

Metaphorically step forward in time and imagine you have achieved your outcome.

Notice what you can see, notice what you can hear yourself and others saying, and notice how you feel.

In effect you are creating a sensory rich "future memory" – and, as sensory rich beings, that's a powerful thing to do.

This is a technique called "creative visualisation" and is something used by successful leaders across the world.

Read the W is for Well Formed Outcomes: Using your Imagination Pearl of Wisdom to learn more about this.

4. Fact find

Gain as much information upfront as you can for the impending or likely situations you have identified.

When fact finding it is important to remain objective and collect data – leave any preconceptions and judgments out of the equation.

5. **Resources**

What are you going to need to achieve your outcome in terms of resources?

Think about the skills you need, the support from other people, materials and tools.

Also think about internal resources – how do you need to be to achieve your outcome in terms of your internal state (e.g. confident, relaxed, energised, open-minded, assertive).

Remember a time when you've had that internal resource and what it felt like to have it.

Draw on that memory to recall the feeling.

6. **Be assertive in your response**

One internal state that is imperative in ensuring you do not become tongue-tied is assertiveness.

You need to think about your communication in terms of the words you use, the tone of voice you use and the body language you use.

You can read more about being assertive in the A is for Assertive Pearl of Wisdom.

Be open, honest and to the point (I like to say "seal it with a KISS" Keep It Short & Simple *which you can read more about in the K is for KISS Pearl of Wisdom*).

Focus on problem solving, moving forward and thinking about the future.

With regard to an assertive tone (the Vocal element of communication) think about how you say the words ("speak the meaning not just the words"), use evenly spaced words and a steady pace.

With body language (the Visual element of communication), ensure your eye contact is direct, relaxed and gentle and keep your posture upright and balanced (with your feet "planted" firmly on the ground).

7.   Believe in yourself

Henry Ford (founder of the Ford Motor Company) said "If you believe you can or believe you cannot, either way you are likely to be right."

Understanding the power of your own thinking and "tapping" into your mind − believing in yourself − is imperative to your overall success.

You can read more about this in the B is for Belief Pearl of Wisdom.

8.   Learn from every experience and opportunity

Use every situation as a learning opportunity by feeding back to yourself.

If you were faced with a similar situation, knowing what you know now (for hindsight is a great thing) ask yourself:

- What would you do more of?

- What would you do less of?

- What would you continue doing?

- What would you stop doing?

- What would you start doing? "

The 'R' Pearl:

> *"Want to go really fast?*
> *Slow down and focus."*
> *Tim Fargo*

"I don't need these"   Few Peeps©

S is for SWOT

S is for... SWOT

SWOT is an acronym and it stands for Strengths, Weaknesses, Opportunities and Threats.

A SWOT analysis is normally conducted on an industry or organisational level to help a business identify their strategy.

In this Pearl of Wisdom we're going to learn about Personal SWOT. This is a fantastic way of gaining a snapshot of "you" at a moment in time. The resulting information can be hugely insightful and useful for you to give yourself feedback as to "what next".

It's an exercise that I use with one-to-one coachees – PAs/EAs regularly come to be when they're at a crossroads in their careers and they need and want clarity on where they are and where they are going. The Strengths and Weaknesses boxes are also fantastic to use for input on your CV or in preparation for an interview too.

How often should I conduct a Personal SWOT?

It is good practice to conduct a regular personal SWOT. This is not a "one-off exercise". Change is constant and I'd recommend conducting a Personal SWOT as a check in with yourself every 2-3 months – or more frequently if you know there have been noticeable or significant changes in your life – or like my coachees, you are at a crossroads in your life.

What considerations do I need to make?

The exercise should take about 30 minutes tops and I recommend you do it all in one go without any distractions so that you're able to remain focussed on answering the questions as one complete package – because one question posed may impact another.

Pick a time and place where you aren't going to be interrupted or disrupted. Think of this as "quality you time" – an investment in yourself. I suggest you grab a cup of tea or coffee or whatever tipple you fancy! plus a big piece of paper and if you're a visual learner some coloured pens.

Separate your paper into 4 squares labelled up S, W, O and T. If you're visual you can use different coloured pens that represent the quadrants here. So you may use Red for Strengths or indeed Red for Weaknesses – whatever works for you.

There are psychological benefits to writing things down too. You've thought of something to write so from your thoughts in your head, you put that down on paper, you add movement by writing it down and then you're reading it as your write so reinforcing the words – it's a multi-sensory learning experience.

Date your Personal SWOT so when you look at it again you know when you did it and can compare it to your new or subsequent SWOTs.

When you're answering a question jot down the first things that come into your mind.

Don't overthink a question and if a question doesn't sound right, look right or feel right just move on to the next question.

Consider yourself as a "whole person" – by that I mean not just you at work. There are things that you will have achieved outside of work that you will be really proud of – perhaps it's raising a happy, healthy child or running a marathon. Your achievements (often outside of work) are gained by drawing on strengths that are part and parcel of YOU so it's important to identify those strengths in your Strengths Box.

How can I use my Personal SWOT for my CV and interview?

The strengths box can be invaluable for writing the "personal statement" section of your CV. It can also give you a boost of self-confidence when you identify "I'm really good at event management or I'm really good at persuading others" – its empowering to take ownership of your strengths.

I do absolutely appreciate that some people struggle with identifying their strengths – we can be really good at giving ourselves "negative feedback" but feel like we're bragging or being big-headed when we say "I'm really good at ... something". But this isn't bragging - it's stating fact and being proud that you good at something. So, when an interviewer asks what your particular strengths are, share them!

For each of your strengths you've identified have evidence ready at interview. So, if one of your strengths is event management for example, you may say – "I organised last month's sales conference for 200 people and 90% of the feedback was a 5 star rating".

Also, if you really do struggle with answering in the first person particularly for the Strengths box, imagine you could clone yourself. So if I was doing a Personal SWOT, I'd ask "what has Lindsay achieved in her life that she is really proud of... Or what are Lindsay's strengths in terms of her personality". This can remove the emotional attachment for the process. What I would say is afterwards repeat those questions answering in the first person – you will probably then find it a lot easier the second, third or subsequent times around!

The Weaknesses box is an interesting one – when I ask the question "by eliminating your weaknesses could these lead to opportunities for you" – there is one answer which is "yes". However, this question is followed up with "are there weaknesses that you're comfortable with that you don't necessarily want to change?". So, in my Weaknesses box I would put "finance" and "maths" or "numerical work" as my weaknesses – I jokingly share with people that once I've run out of counting on my fingers and toes I'm out! I exaggerate I know – I could improve my finance and mathematic prowess and knowledge. However, I get by just fine and it hasn't held me back from achieving and I don't get excited by figures and numbers so I wouldn't be motivated to do this anyway – at the moment anyway. Because I regularly do a Personal SWOT to check in with myself of course...

For the weaknesses I do want to change – to ensure they lead to opportunities – I need to give myself great feedback as to what to do next. Another weakness for me would be the use of Excel, so I'm starting an online course next month to become better at using this.

If an interviewer asks you to identify one of your weaknesses you can still turn this into a positive "I'm not particularly great at using Excel, however I am starting an Excel course next month so I can improve my skills".

What are the Personal SWOT Questions?

Strengths

Use the PAS model.

P =   Personality:

What personality traits do you consider to be your strengths? What tells you that? What evidence do you have to support this? What personality traits do others consider to be your strengths? What feedback/comments have you had from others?

A =   Attributes:

What attributes and skills do you consider to be your strengths? What tells you that? What evidence do you have to support this? What attributes and skills do others consider to be your strengths? What feedback/comments have you had from others?

S =   Successes:

What successes do you have? What achievements are you most proud of? What strengths have you had to draw on to achieve these things?

What networks are you part of? What connections do you have with influential people?

Weaknesses

Consider your weaknesses as areas that potentially you can develop – they are opportunities for you to better yourself.

What personality traits do you consider to be your weaknesses? What tells you that? What evidence do you have to support this? What personality traits do others consider to be your weaknesses? Do you have personality traits that hold you back?

What attributes and skills do you consider to be your weaknesses? What tells you that? What attributes and skills do others consider to be your weaknesses?

What tasks do you avoid because you don't feel confident doing them?

How confident are you in regard to your education and training – are there any weaknesses here? Do you have any "negative" habits?

Opportunities

What networking events, educational classes, training and conferences can you attend? How could you find out about these?

Can you cover for someone on leave or make yourself available to run a project or learn new skills? Do your identified strengths open up any possibilities and opportunities?

By eliminating your weaknesses, does this open up opportunities and possibilities for you?

Which weaknesses do you want (or need) to eliminate to make them opportunities? Which weaknesses are you comfortable with?

Is there any new technology that you can take advantage of?

Are there any trends in your company, sector or profession that you can take advantage of?

Is there a need in your company, industry or profession that no-one is filling?

Threats

What obstacles or barriers do you currently face that could be threatening your success?

Does changing technology threaten your position?

Is your job changing?

Could any of your weaknesses lead to threats?

The 'S' Pearl:

> *"When the winds of change blow, some people build walls and others build windmills."*
> **Chinese Proverb**

"Waiting in Departures"   Few Peeps©

T is for Time

T is for... Time

If you have an assumption that I'm going to share with you all the skills of time management, you are mistaken. For, I feel this would be an imitation Pearl, regurgitating the learning that is already available to you. My recommendation to you for time management expertise is to read Stephen R Covey's "**7 Habits of Highly Effective People**". You'll gain some amazing insights in to those individuals who are the most personally effective and who can prioritise their workload in terms of urgency and importance.

What I'm going to share with you is more of a "Time Travel" Pearl based on a blog post I wrote for www.wearethecity.com – an amazing resource that I'm proud to support.

What would Granny say?

There was something very romantic and magical about travelling back in time with Granny. At the age of about ten I remember asking Granny to share stories of 'The Olden Days'. Stood in the tiny galley kitchen of her Berkshire home, Granny worked through the archives of her memories whilst dunking and poking the steaming washing in the twin tub with a long handled wooden spoon.

Washing days were a major operation at Granny's house – the twin tub was hauled in to position in the middle of the kitchen, the room filled with steam and the stories my Granny shared took on a dreamy quality in the resulting clouds of air that surrounded us.

One of the Bletchley code breakers, my Granny had a secretive smile when recalling the 'war years'. She shared stories of her fellow workers including an aristocratic Lady whose facial beauty was legendary but who was 'cursed with thick black hairs on her legs' (my granny's words not mine!). Granny re-lived evenings preparing for tea dances and grand balls where gravy browning was used to colour your legs and drawing a line of kohl down the back gave the illusion of wearing stockings, when large pots of petroleum jelly took pride of place on the dressing table and the jelly was worked on to your eyelashes in place of mascara .... And always, always my Granny would finish the stories with damp eyes – but not from the steam of the washing.

Recalling these memories now as an adult, I feel a connection across time with my Granny and an appreciation of the nostalgia she must have been feeling as she recalled those war days. She was highly intelligent (hence being at Bletchley Park) and had felt valued at that time in using her intelligence. But when the war ended, like many other females of the time, she slotted back in to society's expectation of her – a stay-at-home wife and mother, running a household, caring for her working husband and hauling the twin tub in to position on wash days with resulting damp eyes.

I wonder – if we could bring Granny back now, what would she think about the women who are leaders and role models in today's society?

What advice would this intelligent woman give to me, her granddaughter, as I juggle the demands of being a Director of my own company with the demands of being a wife, mum, sister, daughter, friend and colleague?

I'm certain Granny would break through the "coding" of society's expectations of women that exist even today, and I'm certain her advice would echo the feedback I give to my female clients.

"The thing that is holding You back from being The Most Successful – is actually You" she would say. "You have so many opportunities to take advantage of". Then she would scroll through her Twitter feed of motivational quotes and Retweet her favourite "Teach your daughter to worry less about fitting into glass slippers and more about shattering glass ceilings", she'd say.

"Realise that your self-belief is your Enigma".

The 'T' Pearl:

> *"Every second, every minute, every hour, every day is yours to shape your future. Only time will tell if you've used it wisely."*
> *Nick Fewings*

"Shoreline stretch"   Few Peeps©

U is for Understanding your power as a PA

U is for...Understanding your power as a PA

As a specialist PA coach and trainer, I meet and work with PAs from different industry sectors and organisations.

As a former PA myself I also have first-hand knowledge of the role and I appreciate the diversity of the job and the challenges you face.

As a fun exercise to "kick start" many of my training sessions my PA clients collate information in an A-Z format to answer the questions **"what are you involved in doing?"** and **"what skills and attributes are needed to be an excellent PA?"**.

I've been running this exercise for several years now and have a pretty extensive – and impressive – list!

It is a sad fact that many PAs underestimate the value of their positions– they don't appreciate or understand the power that they actually have in their roles.

For many of you, the barrier to your success as PA is – well – You.

Fostering and nurturing self-belief and gaining a greater understanding of yourself is at the foundation of all of my training sessions and the A-Z Collation exercise is just one way of helping a PA understand their power.

The A-Z exercise is very often the first opportunity PAs have had to spend quality thinking time really getting to grips with what the PA role is all about.

What is evident from the exercise is that the PA is working at a high level in the organisation, they need to be adept at communicating with Directors, Stakeholders, fellow team members and PAs, clients, customers and visitors. They are privy to lots of information with discretion, integrity and professionalism key when this information is confidential and not yet available to their fellow employees.

For many PAs the exercise is a "light bulb moment" for them, a realisation of the varied and diverse roles they perform and it highlights that they are crucial to the running of their organisations.

The exercise also demonstrates that the expectations of a PA in one organisation can differ greatly to that at another organisation. Indeed, a PAs role can be directly determined by the department or Director he or she is working with.

It is absolutely true that there is no "one size fits all" job specification because of the very nature of the role and I personally don't think we would be adding any value by pushing for a standardised job specification.

Our emphasis needs to be that each PA has a current job specification that absolutely articulates and clarifies what they are involved in doing and the PA has an open, honest communication with their Director to agree their job purpose – you must know what is "in" and what is "out" and what you can be working on that will add the most value for you, your Director and ultimately your organisation.

By doing so you can then maintain those work boundaries and ultimately push back and say "no" *(you can read more in the H is for Helpful Pearl of Wisdom)* to ensure your credibility and professionalism in the workplace.

The 'U' Pearl:

> *"A bird sitting on a tree is never afraid of the branch breaking, because her trust is not on the branch but on her own wings.*
> *Always believe in yourself."*
> *Anonymous*

"Are you listening to me?"   Few Peeps©

V is for Voice

V is for... Voice

Consider your position as a PA as highly privileged. The very nature of your role means you are privy to lots of company information, information that can be sensitive and confidential in nature. Very often you are first "in the know" on business matters ahead of your team members. Your privileged position throws up challenges in the form of knowing when to impart and share information and when not to impart and share information. Discretion and professional integrity rank high on your list of essential skills.

It makes sense that with your privileged position and being "in the know" you are ideally placed and suited to share your opinion and to be a voice in your organisation.

But how do you ensure your voice is heard, and valued, in your workplace?

Ask away

Sharing your opinion is, in effect, providing feedback. The highest quality feedback is offered to the listener. Your very first step in being a voice and sharing your opinion needs to be the question "Is it okay if I share my opinion with you?".

This gets the attention of the person you are delivering your opinion to and their "okay" and "seal of approval" that you can now go ahead with voicing your opinion.

You can also add kudos and credibility to your opinion by reminding your listener that you are in a privileged position. Imagine you've been involved in a new company initiative that your manager has instigated. You've been in the privileged position of knowing what's going on in the managerial world and also "on the floor" in terms of team members putting the initiative in to practice.

You could add some choice words here like "I'm sure you appreciate I've been heavily involved in this project and have been able to observe things not only from your perspective as a manager but also in terms of the team who have implemented it – so it is okay if I share my opinion with you?".

Use the 7, 38, 55 rule

Remember Mehrabian's research introduced to you in the A is for Assertiveness Pearl of Wisdom.

You can have a wonderful "script" ready to share (that's your 7% Verbal element) but unless you pay attention to "how" you deliver your message, in the tone of voice you use (the 38% Vocal element) and how you look when you deliver it (55% Visual element), those words will be diluted.

Make sure you use the 3Vs to deliver the most impactful message.

Practice makes perfect

Practise your message. Ask a friend or a colleague to help you out by pretending to be the person you are going to deliver your message to. Ask your friend for feedback – how well did your opinion come across? Did you use words, tone and body language to full effect? Could you add anything to make it more impactful?

If your message is of a sensitive nature and you can't practice with a friend or colleague, deliver your message in front of a full length mirror and give yourself feedback – remembering that the very best feedback is open and honest. *You can read more on Feedback to Self by reading Pearl of Wisdom F is for Feedback to Self.*

Be Empathetic

Remember, not everyone will have the same opinion as you – that's what makes the world (and the workplace) such an exciting place to be. That's what makes the world (and the workplace) such a challenging place to be! *You can read more about Empathy on Pearl of Wisdom E is for Empathy.*

The 'V' Pearl:

> *"Words mean more than what is set down on paper. It takes the human voice to infuse them with deeper meaning."*
> *Maya Angelou*

" Sole food, food for the soul"

Few Peeps©

W is for Well Formed Outcomes

W is for... Well Formed Outcomes : Using your Imagination

"Your imagination is your preview to life's coming attractions" Albert Einstein.

As many of you know, I'm a Practitioner of NLP – Neuro Linguistic Programming – and share learning with an emphasis on our ability to think differently and act differently to make a difference to our lives.

Our company name, Your Excellency, really sums up what we are about – the learning and development Programmes we provide are about you being excellent at whatever you need or want to do or be. It's all about Your Excellency.

Re-read the B is for Beliefs Pearls of Wisdom. Understand the power of your own thinking. The benefit of "tapping" into your own mind can be highly beneficial, indeed a necessity, in being excellent in your life and achieving all the things you want or need to achieve.

"Memory and imagination have the same neurological circuits, they potentially have the same impact".

When you imagine something, you are creating "a future memory".

This is something that you can work towards – a reference point.

A great colleague once told me that "energy flows where the attention goes". Very simply, you are more likely to achieve the very thing you are imagining.

An example of putting this power of imagination in to practice is when implementing the "Well Formed Outcomes" model to ensure you can, and will, achieve your outcomes, goals and objectives.

The Well Formed Outcome Model

Successful outcome thinking is based on establishing what you really DO WANT. If you listen to people you will often hear them talking about what they don't want. "I don't want to be overweight". "I don't want to have a holiday in rainy England anymore."

This type of thinking is called "away from" thinking. When we make these "don't want" statements our mind creates a representation of the very thing we do not want.

Similarly, by thinking about what we do want our mind will create a representation and start to recognise it.

This type of thinking is called "towards thinking" – establishing what you "do want" enables us to be motivated, clear and precise and it can give us a sense of direction or movement.

Every day we create goals and objectives for ourselves. Sometimes these are things just to get us through the day such as being on time or working through our "to do" list. Sometimes our goals and objectives are of a much more strategic nature and are aimed at creating longer term ambitions or even fulfilling dreams.

We may have been taught to create SMART goals – Specific, Measurable, Achievable, Realistic and Time-bound.

The Well Formed Outcome technique enables you to make your everyday and strategic outcomes even SMARTer. By using your senses to design your outcomes you can ensure they become truly motivational and Well Formed.

The process in simple terms is a checklist allowing you to test and adjust your outcome through a series of self-questioning.

- ### *Is the outcome stated in the positive?*

  The outcome must be expressed in "towards" language, not "away from", e.g. the person that does not want to be overweight would turn their "away from" statement to a "towards" statement "I want to weigh 145 pounds by Christmas 2023".

- ### *Is it self-initiated, maintained and within my control?*

  The outcome must be up to you. Does the outcome rely solely on you or are others going to influence actions and events which you have no control over? If so, then your outcome may need adjusting accordingly.

- ### *Is it sensory specific? (see, hear, feel it)*

  This involves imagining yourself with your outcome complete at some future point. Project yourself forward and act as if it has already happened.

Notice what you can see, notice what you hear yourself and others saying and notice how you feel.

This gives your mind a reference point of what you want to achieve. If you can see, hear and feel it and everything is congruent then your projected outcome is right for you.

• ***What is the context?***

These are the specifics around your outcome with regard to what, where, when and with whom.

Set some realistic frames around what you are aiming for. Is it work, home and/or life in general?

• ***How does it fit?***

How does this outcome fit with your whole life? What is the effect on other people's lives? Is this acceptable to you? What other ecologies are created? By achieving this outcome what else do you lose or disrupt?

This is known as "secondary gain" – what you get by keeping yourself in your current position.

You therefore need to determine where the greater benefits lie – in your current position or by achieving your new Well Formed Outcome.

• ***What internal and external resources are required?***

These may be skills, time, internal states (e.g. confident, relaxed, energised, open-minded) or other people's support, remembering that they need to be within your control and self-maintainable.

- **<u>*What is the desirability now?*</u>**

  Based on the previous checklists and feedback and adjustments required, do you absolutely still want this outcome?

- **<u>*What is the first step?*</u>**

  So, you are ready to do it. What specifically will you do within the next 24 – 48 hours to start to move towards your Well Formed Outcome?

Well Formed Outcomes

The 'W' Pearl:

> *"If you can dream it, you can do it."*
> *Walt Disney*

Few Peeps©

X is for X Marks The Spot

X is for... X marks the spot – how to uncover your personal treasure

In my work as a personal coach I help individuals identify what's important to them – what motivates them, what puts a smile on their face and what gives them that sense of satisfaction.

In essence I like to think about this as helping individuals identify their "map of the world" marked-up with the all-important "X" as a marker for uncovering personal treasure.

I believe that very often we fail to include time in our busy schedules for "quality thinking time".

We may feel that we need to be physically active and physically moving to be "achieving".

However, without quality thinking time – we could be moving in the wrong direction.

When our minds are active rather than our bodies, when we set aside time for quality-thinking and answering thought-provoking questions, we can identify what is important to us, where we are, where we are going and how we are going to get there.

And the knock-on effect of this quality thinking time is that our physical movement is more likely to be in the right direction, the best direction for us personally and we can ensure we are involved in activities that meet what is important to us.

We can identify our own treasure map marked-up with the all-important X that signifies our own personal treasure.

Consider the number of hours you spend in your work environment – you need to be "getting" all the things that are important to you in order to be the happiest, most satisfied and motivated.

So, our first step is identifying what those things actually are.

Set aside some quality thinking time for yourself and put in to practice this useful exercise which I shared with a recent coaching client.

I met with a coaching client the other week who has recently started a new position as a Private PA to a HNWI (High Net Worth Individual) –when they secured the role they were incredibly excited about it.

However, two months in to that role, they contacted me because they felt "something was missing" and wanted to identify what that "something" was.

We spent 30 minutes of quality thinking time.

I asked my client, if they could write an ideal job advert, what would it include?

My client identified the following in their ideal job advert

1	An opportunity to be creative (writing articles, blog posts)
2	A friendly, team environment

3	Opportunities to pull together PowerPoint presentations
4	Booking complex travel itineraries

We numbered these "criteria" and then I asked my client to compare them as follows, giving one "point" for the criteria that was most important in each case

- Compare 1 to 2, 1 to 3, 1 to 4
- Compare 2 to 3 and 2 to 4
- Compare 3 to 4.

We ended up with points assigned as follows:

1	An opportunity to be creative (writing articles, blog posts)	1	(1 point)
2	A friendly, team environment	111	(3 points)
3	Opportunities to pull together PowerPoint presentations		(0 points)
4	Booking complex travel itineraries	11	(2 points)

So in order of criteria and what was important to my client, their own personal treasure is:

2	A friendly, team environment	3 points
4	Booking complex travel itineraries	2 points

| 1 | An opportunity to be creative (writing articles, blog posts) | 1 point |
| 3 | Opportunities to pull together PowerPoint presentations | 0 points |

Now I asked my client in their current role working for the HNWI whether these things were being "met".

Whilst being involved in complex travel itineraries, writing articles and pulling together PowerPoint presentations, the "friendly, team environment" – at the very top of the criteria – was not being met.

The position involved the PA working from the individual's private home office, very often alone (as the HNWI was away on the very well organised complex travel itineraries!).

The most important of my PA client's personal treasure was not being met in her current role – the "something" that was missing for her being the most happy, satisfied and motivated had been identified.

Had my client conducted this exercise prior to securing her current job role she may have thought more carefully about accepting a position that did not meet with her criteria, that did not give her the personal treasures she needs.

And for those of you who want to know the latest on my client, she had an open, honest conversation with the HNWI and shared with him that she needed a different working environment to be happy – they parted on good terms and just this morning she called me to say she had accepted a new position as a PA to

the Marketing Director at a magazine publishers in
London – working in a small, friendly office
environment.

The 'X' Pearl:

> *"What did you do as a child
> that made the hours pass like
> minutes?
> Herein lies the key to your
> earthly pursuits."*
> *Carl Jung*

"Reflection Time"   Few Peeps©

Y is for You

Y is for... You!

Many of the Pearls of Wisdom in this book have introduced you to techniques, tools, models (call them what you will) which you can put into practice to be the very best you can be, so that you can achieve excellence in whatever you do.

One resounding message is that PAs need to be adaptable and flexible in their working styles.

As PAs we need an awareness of how we and others "tick".

We need to tailor how we work to suit our managers and our team, to ensure we get the very best out of ourselves and others.

I do feel I should put a "health warning" on this book though – for my intention is not to produce a robotic production line of cloned PAs.

This de-humanisation of you as individuals is not the purpose of sharing these Pearls of Wisdom.

As I type this, I am all too aware of the journalistic scare-mongering rearing its head in the form of articles that tell us our profession will be redundant.

As technology advances, we are told the work we do can be replaced by robots, AI and apps (and of course, it can be done more efficiently negating the human-errors that inevitably do occur).

I abhorrently do not believe this.

For relationships are at the heart of any successful organisation and human contact will never be replaced by insensitive and characterless apps and robots.

Right at the very beginning of this book I acknowledged that the role of the PA is challenging and demanding – you are very often working with different (strong) characters in your organisations – this is what makes the workplace (and the world!) so challenging.

It is also what makes the workplace so exciting.

We are all unique.

We need to value this diversity.

My message to you is that, with all the great knowledge gleaned from these Pearls of Wisdom, you put them into practice but ensure you do not lose You.

A self-confident boost for You –

The PAS Model

Think about PAS as an acronym for

> Personality
> Attributes and
> Successes.

A great exercise to boost your self-confidence is to identify your top 3 Personality traits, your top 3 Attributes and your top 3 Successes.

Make a note of these.

You can also apply the PAS model to identify your weaknesses and areas that you want or need to work on to progress in your career.

Remember the very best feedback is open, honest feedback!

The 'Y' Pearl:

> *"Today you are You, that is*
> *truer than true.*
> *There is no one alive who is*
> *Youer than You."*
> *Dr Seuss*

"About to spring into action"   Few Peeps©

Z is for Zealous

Z is for... Zealous!

Okay, I admit it. Finding a word that began with Z that fitted with us as PAs was a little challenging – I toyed with the idea of writing about zzzzzz's and getting enough sleep in our profession (based on the M is for Manage your Energy Pearl of Wisdom) but then decided on Zealous because (she says, flicking though her Roget's Thesaurus – the old fashioned way... ...) it means

Devoted	Diligent
Dedicated	Enthusiastic
Eager and	Passionate

and I can imagine you all nodding now in agreement with those words being synonymous with the PA profession!

In fact the word "Zealous" appears on my A-Z collation document of the Executive PA. Just when I think I have a "complete" list, I meet and work with another PA client who adds their own words and input!

So, I want to end this book with that collation sheet. I would so love to see you all reading this and nodding your heads in agreement at this true reflection of The Executive PA!

	What is the role of the Executive PA? What are you involved in doing?	What are the skills & attributes of the Executive PA?
A	Agendas Answering the phone Assisting & Supporting management in achieving their objectives Ambassador for your organisation Ambassador for the PA profession	Assertiveness Asks great questions Able to work with different personalities / deal with different people Adaptable Approach Articulate Accurate Amiable Awareness of manager's objectives, company's objectives + own objectives Awareness of the industry in which you work
B	Booking hotels / meeting rooms Business Planning Budgets Bank Statements / Reconciliations Board Meetings	Build or develop someone else's ideas Being a "buffer" (gatekeeper or gateway) Bonding Building the team

	What is the role of the Executive PA? What are you involved in doing?	What are the skills & attributes of the Executive PA?
C	Communicating effectively with people at all levels, internally and externally Co-ordinating – whereabouts, time management of team, resources Catering Colleague Interaction Committee Meetings Customer / Client facing & liaison Controlling Coaching Contingency Planning (Plan A-Z!)	Concentrates on what "can" be done rather than what "can't" be done Clear about what you want – using "I" statements Co-operative Committed Commercial & Business awareness Confidence (in own ability!) Coaching Courageous Collaborator Curious (the foundation to all learning)
D	Diary management Database management Distribution of mail Delegate tasks Documentation	Diligent Determine Priorities Deadlines (work to them and gain clarity on them) Discreet Dos & Don'ts

	What is the role of the Executive PA? What are you involved in doing?	What are the skills & attributes of the Executive PA?
	Decision Maker Delivering Development	Decisive Dynamic Driven Due Diligence
E	Event management Effective planning Email Management Expenses Evaluate Educate Excel Spreadsheets Editing	Effective communicator Enthusiastic Effective planner Engaged Engaging Eloquent Establishing needs & wants Empathy EI (Emotional Intelligence)
F	Filing Fact finding Filter information (gatekeeper)	Fact-finding Focus on what is relevant in a situation Flexible

	What is the role of the Executive PA? What are you involved in doing?	What are the skills & attributes of the Executive PA?
	Finance	Forward thinking
		Filter
		Fun
		Friendly
		Feedback – can give & receive
G	Gaining / getting information	Give & receive feedback
	Gatekeeper OR Gateway	Goal orientated
	Governance	Great at whatever you do!!
	Good Practice	Gateway
	Geographically aware	Grounded
	Gifts	Generous
	Guests	
H	Hotel bookings	Honest
	Help team and organisation achieve objectives / aims effectively	Helps others express their feelings
		Helpful
	HR	Happy

	What is the role of the Executive PA? What are you involved in doing?	What are the skills & attributes of the Executive PA?
	Hospitality	Hands-on approach
		Hardworking
I	Increasing the output of the team by effective planning, organising and controlling time and other resources	Integrity
		In depth knowledge of the organisation (Vision & Mission Statements, ethos)
	Implement (and maintain) systems and procedures for managing daily workload and keeping track of tasks	Inventive
		Information Source
		Initiative
	IT	Intuitive
	Interviews	Interpersonal skills
	Invoices	Intelligence
		Independent worker
		Ideas generator
		Inspirational
		Inspired
		IT literate

	What is the role of the Executive PA? What are you involved in doing?	What are the skills & attributes of the Executive PA?
		Innovative
J	Juggling the demands of more than one "boss"	Juggler! Jargon-buster Justifying Judging Joyful
K	Keeping management up to date with what's happening Keeper of the Peace	Knowledge of organisation & industry in which organisation operates Keen Kind Kinship KISS (Keep it Short & Simple)
L	Logging telephone calls Liaison officer Leading Line Management	Listening skills Lenient Logical Liaising

	What is the role of the Executive PA? What are you involved in doing?	What are the skills & attributes of the Executive PA?
	Learning & Development Logistics	Loyal Likeable Lateral Thinking LinkedIn user
M	Managing the time of your management team Maintaining good working practices Minutes of meetings Meeting organising Merging / Managing Diaries Mentoring	Maintain boundaries (can say "no") Motivated & Motivational Methodical Mind-reading Mindful Meticulous Morse Code Reader!
N	Negotiating Note keeper Networking Notify Noticing	Negotiator Nice

	What is the role of the Executive PA? What are you involved in doing?	What are the skills & attributes of the Executive PA?
O	Organising (meetings, conferences, workload....)	Open & Honest in communication
		One Step Ahead
	Ordering – stationery / stock / catering / gifts	Organised
		Observant
	Outlook use	Oral Communication
P	Providing information at the right time so managers can make better decisions more quickly	Puts forwards ideas as suggestions (breeds agreement) as opposed to putting forward ideas as statements!
	Projecting a professional image of the team & the organisation	Prioritisation skills
		Proactive
	Prioritisation	Positive Mental Attitude
	Personal Brand	Patience
	Photocopying	Practical
	Proofreading	Professional
	Presentations (PowerPoint)	Project Management Skills (PRINCE2®)
	Planning	PowerPoint
	Project Management	

	What is the role of the Executive PA? What are you involved in doing?	What are the skills & attributes of the Executive PA?
	Purchase Orders Problem Solving	Perceptual (Positions)
Q	Questioning Queries	Quality Questions & Answers Quiet (knows when to be)
R	Relieving the management team of routine & administrative tasks Running the office so that it functions as a comprehensive information and communication centre for the organisation and its clients Reporting Recruitment Regulations	Recognises people have different views / opinions Reliable Resilient Respectful Robust Resourceful Responsible Reactive Reasoning
S	Shorthand / Speedwriting Strategy	Seeks ideas (which in itself breeds giving ideas)

What is the role of the Executive PA? What are you involved in doing?	What are the skills & attributes of the Executive PA?
Supervision	Supports or agrees with something someone else has said (as opposed to explicitly disagreeing or pointing out the difficulties and snags)
Shredding	Seeks clarification or information
Solving problems	Sense of humour
Supporting Teams	Self-motivated
Spreadsheets	Shares ideas and goals with manager(s) and team
Stationery	Structured
Study	Systematic
Slides	Straight-talking
Social Media	Strategic thinking
	Strict
	Social Awareness
	Sensitivity
	Speed
	SMARTer goal setting

	What is the role of the Executive PA? What are you involved in doing?	What are the skills & attributes of the Executive PA?
T	Timely productive of tasks Typing up reports etc. Training Events Training Needs Travel & Itineraries Tracking	Time Management Team member / team work Trustworthy Tactful Tenacious Together(ness) Twitter user Tech-savvy
U	Understudy Undertaking duties in job remit / spec	Understanding of organisations objectives (and therefore manager's objectives) Understand management styles & motivation United
V	Visions & Values Visitor greeting Vacancies Video Conferencing	Voice (to be heard!) Verbal Vital to the team Versatile

	What is the role of the Executive PA? What are you involved in doing?	What are the skills & attributes of the Executive PA?
	Visio (Org Charts software package)	Vocal
W	Workload Word (Office) Water	Works in partnership with their manager(s) Willing & Able Wise Well Formed Outcomes
X	Xeroxing! EXcellent EXcel spreadsheets	Excel software use Excellent at whatever you do! Exceptional Communication Skills X-ray Vision
Y	Yearly Meetings and appointments	Yourself! Youthful
Z		Zealous Zookeeper Zero Errors Zoned-in / Focused Zippy

And so we end our final pearl, the 'Z' Pearl:

"Life is not a dress rehearsal."
Rose Tremain

About the Author

Lindsay Taylor is the Director of Your Excellency Limited, a learning and development specialist offering professional, accredited Programmes and qualifications for the EA, PA and Administrative Professional.

Lindsay spent 10 years as a PA and EA at organisations in the UK and USA, including Transamerica Corporation the innovative financial services and products provider. She is passionate about raising the profile of the EA and PA professional and is known for her high-energy sessions that cut through the jargon and provide instantly-useable skills.

Highly regarded in the EA and PA community, Lindsay issues weekly "Lunch N Learn" emails which provide free training tips. She also produces a monthly podcast "EA/PA Chataway with Lindsay" featuring top stars and guests from the profession.

Previous delegates and attendees of Lindsay's training have commented:

- *"Lindsay is a brilliant trainer – attentive, engaging and patient with the group, along with her wealth of PA experience which we could all relate to"* PA to CEO (UK)

- *"It has been a delight to work with Lindsay. Our delegates benefitted greatly from her insights, knowledge and experience of the PA role"* Conference Producer (Kuala Lumpur)

- *"Lindsay is a highly supportive coach and trainer. Her workshops are relevant and extremely useful for any assistant who would like to gain awareness and communication techniques for their working and personal lives"* Award Winning PA, Charity Sector (UK)

- *"The energy & passion Lindsay has to deliver a great learning workshop is invaluable. The workshop enabled me to learn more about myself and how I come across to colleagues"* PA to CEO (UK)

- *"I had the pleasure of attending one of Lindsay's workshops in Dubai..... an enjoyable, interactive and fascinating experience. I have already been able to make use of what I learned. I would definitely recommend Lindsay and Your Excellency to give you a training experience that is out of the ordinary."* Office Manager, National Research Foundation (UAE)

- *"A must for all PA's or those working in a 'team' environment. Gives a greater understanding of what makes people tick"* President, Association of Celebrity Assistants (UK)

- *"Best workshop so far – real advice for real people – totally practical and fun"* PA, National Health Service (UK)

- *"One of the most interesting and informative course I have ever done!"* PA, Legal Firm, London (UK)

- *"Lindsay exudes friendly professionalism, teaching instantly useable skills in a down to earth manner"* PA, Private Estate (UK)

Lindsay grew up in Hong Kong and has lived in the UK, France and the USA.

She adores the experience of working in different cultures and meeting new people.

She thrives on being busy – approaching everything she does with energy, drive and a real zest for life.

To contact Lindsay, please visit:

www.yourexcellency.co.uk

Printed in Great Britain
by Amazon

19095913R00088